CLASSICAL COMPOSERS

Wolfgang Amadeus MOZART

by Joanne Mattern
with Consultation by John Viscardi,
Executive Director of Classic Lyric Arts
illustrated by Marilena Perilli

RED CHAIR PRESS
Egremont, Massachusetts

Classical Composers has been produced and published by Red Chair Press Books for Young Readers:
Red Chair Press LLC PO Box 333 South Egremont, MA 01258
www.redchairpress.com

Download a Free Activity Guide on our website.

For more information about Classic Lyric Arts, visit www.classiclyricarts.org.

Names: Mattern, Joanne, 1963- author. | Viscardi, John, consultant. | Perilli, Marilena, illustrator.

Title: Wolfgang Amadeus Mozart / by Joanne Mattern, with consultation by John Viscardi, executive director of Classic Lyric Arts ; illustrated by Marilena Perilli.

Description: Egremont, Massachusetts : Red Chair Press, [2025] | Series: Classical composers | Interest age level: 007-010. | Includes bibliographical references and index. | Summary: Wolfgang Amadeus Mozart (1756–1791), an Austrian composer, prodigy, and prolific musical genius of the Classical era ... Colorful illustrations plus photographs of meaningful sites and settings connect readers to important points in Mozart's history. A timeline and B Sharp sidebars add details to the composer's life story.--Publisher.

Identifiers: ISBN: 978-1-64371-418-9 (LB hardcover) | 978-1-64371-419-6 (paperback) | 978-1-64371-421-9 (S&L ebook) | LCCN: 2024936069

Subjects: LCSH: Mozart, Wolfgang Amadeus, 1756-1791--Juvenile literature. | Composers--Austria-- Biography--Juvenile literature. | CYAC: Mozart, Wolfgang Amadeus, 1756-1791. | Composers--Austria--Biography. | LCGFT: Biographies. | BISAC: JUVENILE NONFICTION / Biography & Autobiography / Music. | JUVENILE NONFICTION / Biography & Autobiography / Performing Arts. | JUVENILE NONFICTION / Music / Classical.

Classification: LCC: ML410.M9 M38 2025 | DDC: 780.92--dc23

Image credits: Cover, pp. 4, 7, 10, 13, 14, 18, 22, 24, 27, 28, 29, 31 © Shutterstock; p 4 ©© Giancarlo Costa/Bridgeman Images; p. 18 © Alinari/Bridgeman Images.

Illustrations: Marilena Perilli

Printed in the United States of America

0425 1P CGF25

Table of Contents

Young and Talented

Many people think Wolfgang Amadeus Mozart (WOLF-gang ah-muh-DAY-us MOTE-zart) was the greatest **composer** who ever lived. Like many other musicians, Mozart began composing music when he was just a child. He went on to become one of the most famous and popular musicians of all time. His musical journey started when he was very young.

Wolfgang was born on January 27, 1756. He was born in Salzburg, Austria. His father, Leopold, was a musician. He worked for the princc of Salzburg.

Wolfgang had an older sister. Her name was Maria Anna, but everyone called her Nannerl. When Nannerl was seven, her father started giving her **clavier** lessons. Three-year-old Wolfgang wanted to play too. So, his father started teaching him as well.

B# **B SHARP:** The name "Amadeus" means "loved by God" in Latin.

Mozart's Birthplace is one of the most visited museums in Austria.

Leopold and his wife saw that little Wolfgang was very talented. When he was six years old, he taught himself to play the violin. He also wrote his first **concerto**. It seemed there was almost nothing with music that young Wolfgang could not do. He was clearly a musical **prodigy** as he was reading and writing music from age five.

Leopold wanted to share Wolfgang and Nannerl's talents with the world. He decided to take the children on tour.

Imagine "writing" music: you would create and play the music first on an instrument, like a piano or clavier or violin. Next you would try to remember each note you played and write those notes on a sheet of paper using the bars and symbols of musical sounds. Then you would play from the music you wrote to be sure no corrections are needed. Now think about Wolfgang doing this at six-years-old!

Wolfgang on Tour

In 1762, Leopold and the children left Salzburg. They traveled all over Europe. The family visited many different cities. Wolfgang and Nannerl gave concerts in every city. They loved to perform. And people loved to hear them play.

The Mozarts also played for **royalty**, a great honor. They played for the royal families in France and England.

B# **B SHARP:** Touring was hard work. The children were often paid with gifts instead of money. Sometimes they weren't paid at all!

Leopold was a good teacher. And Wolfgang loved to learn. He studied the music of many different composers. While he was on tour, he got to meet some of them. Mozart was then able to introduce different musical ideas into the pieces he wrote.

One of the composers Mozart met was Johann Christian Bach. Johann Christian was the son of the great composer Johann Sebastian Bach. Johann Christian and Wolfgang became good friends even though Christian Bach was more than 20 years older than Wolfgang.

A Trip to Italy

After the tour, the Mozarts went back home to Austria. Wolfgang kept writing music. In 1768, when he was 12 years old, Mozart wrote his first **opera**.

Leopold Mozart was proud of his son. He hoped Wolfgang could get a job as a composer in Salzburg. But that did not happen. After all, young Mozart was only 12.

Trouble in Paris

Mozart returned again to Salzburg in 1771. He was now 15 years old. Even though he was young, he got a job in an **orchestra** that performed for the city's archbishop.

Unfortunately, Archbishop Hieronymus von Colloredo and Mozart did not get along. Mozart thought the music the archbishop wanted him to write was boring. The Archbishop got tired of listening to Mozart complain.

Mozart decided to leave Salzburg. In 1777, he and his mother traveled to Paris. His father Leopold said that in Paris, "the fame of a man of great talent echoes through the world." Mozart played many concerts in Paris. He also wrote lots of new music.

Mozart worked hard and earned good money. However, he spent money faster than he could make it. Mozart loved to buy nice, stylish clothes. He bought expensive wigs. And he threw big parties.

Then something terrible happened. Mozart's mother got very sick. In 1778, she died suddenly. Mozart returned home again to Salzburg.

B#

B SHARP: Powdered wigs were high-fashion in the late 1700s. Think about America's Founding Fathers like George Washington.

Love and Music

Mozart went back to work for Archbishop von Colloredo because he needed money. Then the two had another big fight. The archbishop threw Mozart out of the palace. Mozart was tired of Salzburg. He moved to a bigger city called Vienna.

Mozart loved living in Vienna. He performed for Emperor Joseph II. Here he was free to write music that was different than anything else of the time.

B# **B SHARP:** Mozart could hear a tune, then play it again with many **embellishments**.

For a while, Mozart lived with a family named the Webers. He soon fell in love with their daughter, Constanze. On August 4, 1782, Wolfgang and Constanze got married.

Mozart wrote lots of beautiful music in Vienna. He wrote great operas. Some operas, like *Don Giovanni*, were serious. Others, like *The Marriage of Figaro*, had both funny and sad scenes.

B#

B SHARP: One of Mozart's most popular operas was ***The Magic Flute***. It is filled with funny scenes but has some scary parts written into it, too.

Important Dates in Wolfgang Amadeus Mozart's Life

1756 Wolfgang Amadeus Mozart is born in Salzburg, Austria.

1759 Mozart begins playing the clavier.

1762 Mozart's father takes him and his sister on a concert tour of Europe, where he plays for royal families.

1771 Mozart begins working for Salzburg's archbishop.

1777 Mozart and his mother travel to Paris.

1778 Mozart's mother dies.

1781 Mozart moves to Vienna, where he writes some of his most famous works.

1791 Mozart dies on December 5.

Monument in memory of Wolfgang Amadeus Mozart in Burggarten, a public park in Vienna, Austria.

Glossary

clavier a keyboard instrument such as a piano or harpsichord

composer a person who writes music

concertos musical pieces for solo instrument with an orchestra

embellishments notes added to music to give it more decoration and variety in the sound

honors awards that show great respect

opera A story set to music for one or more singers and an orchestra

orchestra a large group of musicians who play together on many different instruments

prodigy a highly talented child or young person

royalty members of the nobility, such as kings, queens, and emperors

symphonies long pieces of music for an orchestra

variations music that includes changes to an original piece of music

Read More About Mozart

McDonough, Yona Zeldis. *Who Was Wolfgang Amadeus Mozart?* Penguin Young Readers, 2003.

Vegara, Maria Isabel Sanchez. *Mozart (Little People, Big Dreams).* Frances Lincoln Books, 2023.

Venezia, Mike. *Wolfgang Amadeus Mozart*. Children's Press, 2017.

Index